CHERYL KNOLL

Copyright © 2024 by Cheryl Knoll.

All rights reserved. No part of this publication may be reproduced, distributed, or transmitted in any form or by any means, including photocopying, recording, or other electronic or mechanical methods, without the prior written permission of the author, except in the case of brief quotations embodied in critical reviews and certain other noncommercial uses permitted by copyright law.

Printed in the United States of America

ISBN 979-8-89114-044-8 (sc)
ISBN 979-8-89114-045-5 (hc)
ISBN 979-8-89114-046-2 (e)

Library of Congress Control Number: 2023924128

2024.02.02

MainSpring Books
5901 W. Century Blvd
Suite 750
Los Angeles, CA, US, 90045

www.mainspringbooks.com

Contents

Hidden Hills 1
What the Flowers Said 3
Him and Her and Love 4
Autumn's Invitation...5
It Happens in the Trees 6
Passion Lake 7
Bad Birth...8
Here He Comes 9
Fight Evil...10
Things Change 11
Caution to the Wind 12
Grown- Up Flower Child 13
The Lark's Song..14
Angels Watching...15
Leaving Happy, Leaving the Sad...16
Tree Care...17
For You Lord 18
Hiding and Healing 19
Come Sweet Soul..20
Be True to You 21
Manly Men 22
Keeping Secrets 23
Socialism, Jerk..24
Not Begging for Crumbs 26
Time to Mourn 27
Make it Rain Love 28

No Other Me	30
Good Advice	31
Bad Neighbor	32
Distracting Sheeple	33
Over Love	35
Surprise on the Road	36
Sad State Fair	37
Time	39
The Cup and the Pail	40
My Choice	42
Frost	43
Mountain Tops	44
Silver to Gold	45
Regrets? (Sure)	46
The Good Sauce	47
Mended Wreck	48
She's God's	50
Home, Where Hearts Live	51
Summoned to the Hills	53
Heart Strings	55
Fig Tree Generation	56
God's Warrior	57
Finding Sheep	59
Chocolates	60
Frank and that Smell	61
Drunkenness	63
Autumn Love	64
He is in Love	65
Eternal Love	66
For Me	67

Hearts Hide Scars	68
Underworld War	69
She's Surfacing	70
Rabbit Talk	71
Time Travel	72
Flower Zone	74
Long Summer	75
Locked Up Hearts	76
No More Politics	77
Sparkling Snow	78
She Changed	79
Wild Hearts	80
Words from Leaves	81
Going Down	82
Falling Rain, Blowing Kisses	83
Freedom Train	84
Driftwood and Diamonds	86
Race to Win	87
Some Books Do Not Open	88
The First Earth Age	89
It Will	90
Winter Fog	91
Bye-Bye Burger Joint	92
Waterfalls	93
Live for Good	94
Their Very First Kiss	95
Dreaming	96
Light in the Fog	98
The Visit	99
Digital Warriors	101

Flying High	103
I Am Who I Am	104
Hall of Same	105
Seasons Change	106
Bad Job Work Week	107
Truth, Light, Love	108
Love Words	109
Thinking Process	110
Somewhere	111
The Right Road	112
We are Only Human	113
Poor Harvest	114
Wrong Love	116
Watching Him	117
Let God Move	118
Caution: Foxes	119
The Light	120
Blackbird Good-byes	121
P's and Q's	122
Baggy Bottoms	123
Self-Centered	124
Swallow Stream	125
Scandalous Rumors	126
Law of Attraction	127
Gifts to Workers	128
After the Rain	129
Patriots vs Traitors	130
Do not Be a Rug	132
What was That?	134
I Need a Scarecrow	135

Outside Aging..136
Sparrows.. 137
Gift to One Hidden 138
Do not Turn Around...139
Good-bye Hidden Hills 140

Hidden Hills

I found myself in the hidden hills
I heard words spoken by daffodils
Suddenly to my surprise
I saw the wildflowers all had eyes

All the flowers were staring at me
I said "take a picture if you want to see
What I look like with a broken heart
Deep down in here, it came apart"

The daffodils were now telling me
"God sees the deep things you cannot see
The pain you feel, He feels it too
It is not only inside of you"

I told the flowers "I know these things
And I know the love from feathered wings
But never real love from a man"
I started crying and then I ran

In unison they all yelled "stop
Please do not let another tear drop
Just stop now, do not run anymore
You see, God is opening another door"

I stopped and there appeared a door
The flowers said "do not cry anymore
Just walk slow and your heart will heal
God's love is all you need to feel"

I know they are right. I know they are right
And all the wildflowers that had sight
Were left with just a picture of me
A reflection of what I used to be

A new door opened and then it closed
The picture of me I was not posed
They can keep their sorry vision of me
With a broken heart only God and flowers can see

I will remember the words the flowers said
And the door that opened and where it led
It was real life in the hidden hills
Where wildflowers talk with daffodils

What the Flowers Said

The flowers looked her over
They studied her troubled face
One flower said "I see you going
On a journey somewhere and someplace

Troubled one, you are going to be fine
We can see you are well on your way
You have a God given purpose to fulfill
You have special messages and words you must say

Remember just like choosing flowers
Give particular care when choosing words
There is a depth and beauty to capture
Like catching beautiful wild flying birds

When you speak of love reach deep inside
Try to find those feelings you are trying to hide"
She said "what is in my heart is what I feel
The love and the broken heart were real"

She studied the flowers and watched flying birds
She said "I know what you are trying to say
The flowers I choose and the birds I will catch
I will do both in my own way"

The flowers said "that is what we want to hear
We are going to miss you, now be on your way dear
Yes, run along, hurry, here comes the night
We see you chose some flowers, now you can write"

Him and Her and Love

When he looked into her eyes
He saw starlight not the lies
And when he felt her soft smooth skin
He felt forgiveness not the sin
Love will walk with blinders on
Where there was a vixen, he saw a fawn
There was only one woman for him
And it was her

When she looked into his eyes
She saw love, she saw the sun rise
And when she felt the strength of his hands
She felt forgiveness that understands
Love is helping her get well
For a time, she was lost, and she has been through hell
She knows there is only one man for her
And it was him

Love will grow and it will root
It will grow branches, blossoms, and fruit
They will both find enough love there
Their love will grow deeper, and they will bear
More love

Autumn's Invitation

Autumn sends its invitation
To trees to dress in fall attire
It sends its message to the flowers
Thank you for coming, you may retire
It tells the grass to slow its growing
It tells the pumpkins go ahead and shine
It tells the gardens you worked so hard
But now the season is mine, all mine
Cooling nights and days grow shorter
Harvest time and corn husks blow
Now is the time to change the season's décor
Autumn, you know how to put on a show

It Happens in the Trees

It happens when I am in the trees
A feeling that comes over me
Calmness and serenity
A power that the eye cannot see

A power on a grander scale
That hung between the tree and nail
Now God's spirit dwells in the trees
The leaves, they whisper in the breeze

Under trees that tower me
Something happens and I see
In God Almighty my roots are deep
My spiritual eyes are not asleep

Rooted in the Word of life
I give no room to worldly strife
Broken limbs and fallen trees
I have dealt with all of these

Trees stand strong and so I try
To stand like trees that I walk by
I feel their strength and say Lord please
Help me stay as strong as the trees

Passion Lake

I stood on the edge of passion lake
It was full of curious feelings
I did not want to cast a line
It might cause my heart new dealings

I thought of putting a flirt on the line
And cast it to a certain spot
On second thought rejection hurts
And I told myself I better not

I could just gaze upon the surface
And watch for anything to move
Then again, I might see my reflection
I would see I have nothing to prove

Sure, I could dive in feet or headfirst
And take my chances on a thrill
The way things always go for me
I might only feel a chill

Since I am here, I will just look
And wonder what could happen here
I will just cast and catch a daydream
I will wait till the water I see is clear

Bad Birth

Critical race theory
You are ugly offspring
Born from Marxism and wayward thinking
Socialism is your nanny
You are swaddled in ragged lies
You are fed spoiled milk
Which you spit up on those who hold you
Your sister ignorance is pushing you in a carriage
Taking you for a stroll to the Teachers union
Of course, you will spit up on them
They will feed it to the students
Crib death is calling for you
Before you crawl then toddle
America's patriots who love our country
Are going to choke you to death
Full throttle

Here He Comes

Here comes the Son of God
We have given Him our lives to hold
We gave Him our hearts and souls
Now he will give us crowns of gold

Here comes the Son of God
We sang our praises over the years
We prayed our thoughts and hearts to Him
He has conquered evil and our fears

Here comes the Son of God
Though life seemed long it was a blink
Now Christ is offering His cup
His cup of life we lived to drink

Here comes the Son of God
Everlasting love He gives
Everlasting life for us
He died for us and now He lives

Fight Evil

Evil gathers and it builds
Evil hides and multiplies
Evil deceives and causes pain
It may shine when in disguise
Evil can grow undetected
Though when it shows it wakens scorn
Righteous people will rise against it
That is how a storm is born
Here comes the storm
The storm to end all storms
We saw it coming now bring it on
We have our gospel armor on
God told us to stand and fight
We slash evil with His might
If you cannot fight, then you can pray
Powerful prayers can make a way
Swathing paths through evil thickets
Come on evil, time to get your tickets
To hell

Things Change

Yesterday the world was mine
I held it firm, and it did shine
I strummed it like a fine guitar
While I watched my guiding star

It was mine I had control
I lived daily from my soul
Staying strong that was a goal
And then I fell into a hole

Today the world is mine no more
My life has gone through sorrows door
The world for me is now the past
Todays' go by they do not last

Tomorrow I will live again
I do not know where, I do not know when
I will find another world to hold
I will turn my sorrow into gold

I will find a new world to be mine
In time my new world will be fine

Caution to the Wind

There it goes
In the wind
Caution
Someone threw caution
To the wind
And it blew away
It left room for nonsense
To settle in
Too much nonsense is tiring
Someone should have been
More cautious
We need to throw politics to the wind
Make sure it is windy
With excessively high gusts

Grown-Up Flower Child

She is a flower lady
A grown-up flower child
She likes tastefully planted flowers
Back then she liked them wild

She has a rock'n flower garden
Big rocks and flowers and metal art
She tries to keep it a little balanced
But she is an old rocker at heart

Tie-dye clothes and flowered crocs
She has a thing for flowers and rocks
She likes to help the birds and the bees
She says "ouch" when on her knees

Rock'n'roll music she hears in her head
It plays while she removes blooms that are dead
When she is done working and hurting, (oh dear)
She sits on the patio and enjoys her cold beer

Flower child, she remembers those days
Bell bottom jeans and the hems adorned frays
With fondness she recalls the flowers in her hair
Now her hair is messy, and she does not care
She is still cool

The Lark's Song

In the dark
I heard a Lark
I said why do you sing at night
The Lark said why
So, I do not cry
For things in this world are not all right
The Lark said people just do not see
They have eyes that they do not use
They walk around with blinders on
They believe the lies they watch on news
Some believe and that is all
They do not let their God love grow
They can barely say God's name
Or live for Him, it is sad, I know
Some do not even believe in God
But you do as I watched him nod
Those like you
There are just a few
Who hold onto God's guiding rod
I sing at night to those with sight
The Lark's sweet song he sang to me
God sends His best
He gives you rest
He blesses you because you see

Angels Watching

Angels are always watching us
They stand before the face of God
They step in and intervene
At times when God gives them a nod
He gives His angels charge over us
They watch to keep us safe and well
Though if they see you doing naughty things
They will put you on God's list for hell

Leaving Happy, Leaving the Sad

Momma, everything looks dark
Will you turn on the light so I can see?
I am feeling better today
Will you stay in my room and sit with me?

Daddy, I am feeling good
I see the angel watching me
That angel makes me feel happy
It is so dark daddy; can you see me?

Oh momma, the angel is singing to me
I know it is the prettiest song I could hear
Do you know the song Momma, so you can sing it too?
A few of the words are "there is no fear"

Momma and daddy, I love you so much
And I am not hurting anymore
The angel said we are going to go home
Look at us walking right through the door

The angel is holding my hand tight
The angel said you will be all right
The angel is happy and so am I
Momma and daddy, I love you, good-bye

Tree Care

Sometimes roots will leave the soil
The tree can still live fine that way
Some roots know where they belong
In the soil or in the light of day
Branches too tired to bear leaves
Might be alive but they will be late
I hope there is some life shown soon
The pruning saw may just not wait
When you are God's tree, He prunes and shapes
Some roots He buries, some He lets be
Sometimes He prunes and that cut can hurt
He knows how to make a beautiful tree

For You Lord

It is not my will but thy will
I live not for me but thee
For living holds no life for me
If I do not live my life for thee
What you want I want it too
You died for me I live for you
Your will is mine, my life is thine
Your love you give, for thee I live

Hiding and Healing

She was wandering the hills
Looking over her hiding places
She was looking for things she put away
She was covering all their traces
She was hiding it all forever
Things never wanting to see again
She was healing and found her place
She did not want to "remember when"

Here the flowers with beautiful faces
Were helping her find the best hiding places
They knew how to make past things go away
With each thing she buried, they joined her to pray
Beautiful birds would drop seeds on the ground
To grow tall
And make sure past things were not found

This part of her journey was healing her heart
Grateful that God's birds and flowers had a part
She was burying bad memories
Now her new ones can live
And they will
When you forget as well as forgive

Come Sweet Soul

Walking out of the dark, one slow step at a time
Your steps will be easier with the first glimpse of light
The path will start glowing under your feet
Stay on it and you can walk out of the night
Come sweet soul
The light is inviting
It is warm with love and shining the way
The illusion of night
Loses its power
When you stay focused on God's light
And pray

Be True to You

Stay true to yourself
Stay true to "everything you"
Your feelings, your thoughts
Your words, your speaking
Do not let others do any tweaking
Stay away from religions
That make you act strange
It will be God who will change you
If he wants you to change
Letting others change you is going to sting
Be yourself, be authentic
Just do your own thing
Do not change to impress people
When you do not like what they do
Stay away, you do not need them
Be happy just being you

Manly Men

Lord, can you find us more manly men
Where are the manly men going?
Where are the men who used to be men?
Without their feminine side showing

This ride to socialism is taking them away
They are taught not to act in a manly way

Do not display your testosterone and do not speak out
Boys are being taught not to be stronger than others
That is how socialist leaders control them
They want them to act more like their mothers

Lord, we need the manly men we lack
We need them to fight and bring morals back
We need them to fight the socialist rule
Not to act like little girls in school

We need manly men to shine your saving light
We need manly fathers to raise their children right
To correct gender lunacy and live with insight
That we will lose our country
If they do not stand up and fight

Lord, please find us more manly men

Keeping Secrets

If the stars could keep a secret
I would tell them of my heart
The hidden things I keep from others
I want to speak but cannot start
I just look up to the stars
And wish I could confide my words
But stars just cannot keep those secrets
With excitement they like to tell the birds
You know birds they like to chatter
Of good they sing and of sad they peep
The stars confided in the wrong ones
There are no secrets birds can keep
I will keep my secrets locked inside
I will tell the stars and birds no more
It is enough for me that God knows
I will gaze at stars that is what they are for

Socialism, Jerk

To my dear friend do not be a jerk
Socialism fails it does not work
If you are a socialist, you will be poor
If you work, your money is not yours anymore
Your money they say will help the poor
Well, that is hilarious you are the poor
The poor you help are really the wealthy
The rich people's wealth is extremely healthy
A tiny group are wealthy, the masses are poor
You decide you do not want socialism anymore

It is too late friend and now you will see
You are powerless living in poverty
You will not have anything, and you will wonder why
You believed the promises, you believed the lie

They will tell you the government is your friend
They will take care of you until your end
You will not have to work, we will pay your way
We will all be the same someday
Fake promises they cannot keep
You will be so hungry that you cannot sleep
You will find they have taken all your rights
Now you are living with sleepless nights

You will be hungry, there is little to eat
You will be thin, looking out on the street
You will be looking for something good to come
You wanted socialism, gee you were dumb
That is what wonderful socialism will bring
It is your fault you did not want freedom to ring
You were duped into socialist lies
That is why you are living in garbage and flies

Dear friend you wanted everything free, free, free
Free healthcare free school free money no work
All the free stuff came with a price
No more freedom because you wanted socialism you jerk

Not Begging for Crumbs

She felt as though she was begging for crumbs
Liking someone and wanting to be friends
She did not know what people wanted from her
Before it gets started the friendship ends

She did not want to be a pleaser
Or just a giver while the other takes
She did not want to put on airs
Just to attract fakes

She was not begging for crumbs for sure
She does not care that no one knocks on the door
Trying to be friends should not be a chore
She does not waste time on that anymore

She pleases God now, the past is the past
She is not looking for friends that do not last
Her stride is strong, she holds her head high
She is friends with Jesus, and she is getting by
Simply fine

Time to Mourn

During times of sadness be still
Your loved one comes to mind, you cry
When least expected you smile
While being still you sigh
Mourning is a process it is true
Some say their good-byes and move on
Some hold on a little harder
When their loved one is gone
Some hearts mourn
Be it a little or a lot
Some hearts move on
Some hearts will not

Make it Rain Love

I lived for years being alone
I lived for years not being loved
I had so much love I wanted to give
I had so much love that wanted to live
I did not want to be alone
I wanted a man to call my own
I all but died inside
I all but died inside

What do you do when you have love to give
What happens with your love that wants to live
I prayed to God to ease the pain
I prayed to God to make it rain
Rain on the love that burns inside
Rain on the pain I try to hide
Lord, make it rain, rain, rain
Rain love
Make it rain love on me

God heard me pray
He heard every word I had to say
He answers prayers when we pray
He knows a special man he will send my way
I will love my man
He will love me like no other man can
He will have all the love I have to give

I have so much love for us to live
I will live as though my prayer has come true
I will manifest the love I have for you
God make it rain
God make it rain, rain, rain
Rain love
Make it rain love on me

No Other Me

I recall the past versions of myself
When I was troubled
When I was alone
Some versions I forgot
Some versions I will not own
Once I was carefree and for a time, I was fun
Now I am the real me
My morphing is done
Love planted its roots deep and wide
There are no more versions of me to hide
Now that you love me
I am the best I can be
And when we look at each other
Love is all that we see

Good Advice

She wanted to go someplace
She put on her made up face
She wore clothes that would attract
Looking for the man she lacked
Seems every time she found someone
Turns out he just wanted fun
She did not present her qualities right
When make-up runs it is a sight

She was not taking her mother's advice
Be patient you will find someone nice
Her mother tried to fix her head
Here are the other words she said

Do not be desperate, my doll
You are too good for them all
Do not give in, hold your clothes tight
Do not leave with men just say goodnight
Keep your dignity in check
Do not wear hickies on your neck
Wear clothes with a little more taste
Do not leave bars with men, in haste

Her mother was right, she gave her birth
She wanted her daughter to feel her worth
We can pray to God you meet someone
Who is looking for you and not just fun

Bad Neighbor

I remember
When I first saw that bundle of fur
That puppy ball and I really loved her
I held her and hugged her
We would play on the floor
She woke me up at night to go out the door
I remember I had never loved a puppy like that
The biggest ball of fur that made her look fat
I remember
My dog, she was so good
I gave her the best care like any owner would
I remember
I moved to a farm out of state
Next to a neighbor I would soon hate
I remember
He shot my dog and he lied
The vet could not help her, and my dog died
I remember
He was shooting at me in my own yard
He lied about that too and feelings were hard
I moved off that miserable farm
I did not have to suffer any more harm
He had no kindness for his neighbors next door
I hope God pays him back a hundred times more
He had a pig snout and looked like a hog
Lord, please pay him back fifty times for me
And fifty times for my dog
I still remember

Distracting Sheeple

A spoonful of disaster
Crooked leaders say
We will use it as a tool
To lead people astray

They say people are stupid
Like sheep they will follow
Just keep spoon feeding them lies
They say oh yes, they will swallow

Let us cause some more distraction
We will use racism and hate
And while you are watching riots
They are stealing from your plate

Let us cause more racial tension
We will put actors on TV
If it is on the media
Sheeple believe what they see

Wake up little sheeple
Evil ones like to play
With sleepy little people
They want to rule someday

Go turn off the TV
Mainstream news is fake
No more alphabet networks
It is time to be awake

You stop watching programmed fake news
Go live your life with your own views

Over Love

Oft' I have given thought to love
Elusiveness the game it plays
Some find it abundantly
While I searched it all my days
Hide and seek it toyed my heart
I sought it and it always hid
At times it pitied me a glance
Though never gave my heart a bid
Now love is but an after thought
As I have grown on to other thinking
Finding love is for the young
For me it is wine and a smidge of drinking

Surprise on the Road

Traveling along a road
Up a hill and over a rise
Going along at your own pace
Then you barely believe your eyes
You can see for miles
Miles of land and wide- open skies
The scenery takes your breath away
It is an elevated high
Occasionally life can happen this way
Just day to day living for you
Out of nowhere you get a surprise
There is something new for you to do
Only it is not out of nowhere
God shows you something new
He tries to guide you down your paths
He knows what is best for you
You can stop and take it in
Or you can just move on
That is the secret to opportunities
You take them or they are gone

Sad State Fair

It was time for the sad state fair
There would be no happy people there
There was no laughing or joking or smiles
The only ride was a slow train for miles
There was no carnival food
Just coffee and bread
The only exhibits were animals...dead
There were no booths with games to play
No pretty colors, everyone wore gray
People walked slow and stared and cried
They could not believe America died

It happened when people stuck their heads in their asses
They were too busy dividing us into races and classes

They believed the lies the ruling class told
They wanted socialism instead of good gold
Socialism grew and gave Communism life
Then Communism took Marxism to wife
USA fighters were overpowered, and now dead
No red, white and blue, now it is just red

The racism lies and plots were fulfilled
Those who pushed it caused millions to be killed
Child rape and murder, child rape and porn
No children left and no more would be born
You see, girls were now boy'd and boys were now girl'd
Those who hated God banned God from the world
The gender agenda was part of Satan's plan
To spite God, he wanted to end woman and man

No more politics, the ruling class ruled
No one had money and no one was schooled
Human flesh is what the ruling class ate
Human flesh...cannibalism, man isn't that great

People were thin, they could not find food
Everyone was sad, there was no other mood
The few of us who prayed, we had to beware
You could not trust anyone, anymore out there
There was no happiness left anywhere
But some people thought we still needed a state fair

Time

Time will tell what will it say?
Of yesterday or of today
It does not speak
But shows its hand
When data and proof
Some demand
You cannot hide
But you can try
Time does not let much slip by
It has a way to no surprise
Revealing the past's
Deeds or lies

The Cup and the Pail

She walked to the mulberry trees
Oddly, she fell to her knees
She saw an angel with a silver cup
He said "do not kneel to me get up

I am a servant just like you
I have come here with a special view
Ready yourself to see wonderful things
I see you looking but I do not have wings

There has been a veil over what is true
It is amazing how you have seen right through
The veil is lifting and what is underneath
Will cause great wailing and gnashing of teeth

The cup of wrath that God will pour
Is a giant vessel, the pouring will roar
Prophetic words you will see God keep
Are going to wake up those who sleep

You see this little cup of mine
I brought you a taste of what will shine
I will hold the cup, you take a drink
A blessing from God for the way you think

It is for your heart, your soul and mind
After you swallow it, you will find
A strength you have never had before
No one will use you anymore"

It is true angels do not have wings
She is looking forward to wonderful things
Her angel was gone, she felt a breeze
He left her pail full of mulberries

My Choice

The word of God my guiding rod
The words I feel
They are God's, they are real
God's words inform
They teach the soul
To live and love God in control
No greater way of life for me
No other choice for me it is clear
The only way to live my life
To keep the word of God right here
God's word grows
It does not die
It does not change
It does not lie
It guides it lives
It loves it gives
God's word endures
It is here for all
It comforts those
Who hear God's call

Frost

Frost can bring the garden down
It can dull the shine on grass
It can hide or blur a vision
When it adheres to outdoor glass
Frost arrives and brings its baggage
Though it bears a beautiful name
Many people are not happy to see it
I still like it just the same
When I am home, it brings a comfort
Frosted glass is nature's design
The garden is done, mowing stopped being fun
My work is done, and it all looks fine
Really, I am happy to see the frost
It lets me know that rest is near
I have had my fill of outdoor work
Frost, I am glad you are finally here

Mountain Tops

Where clouds sit on eagles' nests
So beautiful it could be a dream
In the distance, snow on peaks
Mountain water flows downstream

Rare wildflowers bloom for God
For rarely trod the feet of men
The few that come can barely leave
They say they will return but do not know when

Almighty God, you must rest here
What I feel, there are no words
Your presence I feel in my heart
When I hear songs from mountain birds

It calls to leave humanity
And live a life with God nearby
He who dwells on mountain tops
Will surely live with the most high

Silver to Gold

The sun near setting
I can see the silver road today
Heaven's light is shining on it
A calming light to those on the way
The sides of the road
Reflect light like borders
The road going to heaven
Where one day I will stay

I travel on the silver road
The memories I take are faded and old
The shining silver road I see
So beautiful and it is calling me
This lovely vision is taking hold
It shows itself to those growing old
To those who pray and whose hands fold
Their destiny is eternity
Where the streets are pure gold

Regrets? (Sure)

She had to gather her thoughts
They spilled to her mouth and went willy nilly
She likes to keep them to herself
But she said something that was silly
She liked her thoughts controlled and concealed
She did not want her feelings revealed
She mis-placed her composure so easy and quick
It was not like her, and it made her feel sick

She hoped her silliness was ignored
She spoke of things she should not, oh dear Lord
She knows God works in mysterious ways
But she said something that bothered her for days
She wondered if she said things that needed to be said
No, they were not as she hangs her head
Though God has a way of making things right
She is stronger now and she has more insight

God can make everything work to our good
If we love Him and pray to Him as we should
Her thoughts all gathered and now kept in check
She knows we are all human and fall short
What the heck

The Good Sauce

Mama found a bag of spice
Into the pasta sauce it went
Everyone who ate the sauce
Thought it must be heaven sent

Everyone became euphoric
They were grinning ear to ear
But dad's face had changed suddenly
His eyes now showed a look of fear

He went and looked up in the cupboard
That is where dad kept his weed
Mama found oregano
And made this great spaghetti feed

God made every seed-bearing herb
So, I do not want to judge this case
It is hard to say that this was bad
With smiles and sauce on every face

Mended Wreck

I saw the sign "wrecks mended here"
I shrugged my shoulders; while I am near
Man, I am a wreck, so I walked in
I said to the man, where do I begin?
He asked what I was doing here
I said I am a wreck from too much beer
He said we only mend wrecked cars
Not people who get wrecked in bars

He said I am sorry, you mis-read the sign
I said whatever, I just bought more wine
I said what is a little more drunk to a drunk
I bought some day -old donuts for my wine to dunk

He said lady, I can do something for you
I can help you pray and if your heart is true
If you really want help, bow your head with me
We can pray to God to help you see
He said being drunk is no way to live
You seem like a lady with a lot to give

We prayed to God for His healing touch
I felt it working and I figured as much
I should have come here later in the day
Now I have a bottle of wine to throw away
I will still eat the donuts made yesterday
I will be sure to thank God for them when I pray

It is true I mis-read the sign
But the beautiful prayer to God was mine
It was just for me, and I thought heck
The sign was right, I am a mended wreck

She's God's

She
Can do all things
Through God who strengthens her
She
Has love to give
To those in need and those with fur
She
Gives praise to God
When blessings flow or when they stall
She
Always tries her best
Anytime she feels God call
She
Trusts God
He has always been her guiding light
She
Belongs to God
She knows she is going to be all right

Home, Where Hearts Live

I see home now down the way
The longing to get home today
The welcoming door I see from here
More inviting as I draw near

Home the place where bonded gather
Where childhood memories still live
Family dialog and inquiries
And our opinions we force or give

Judgement takes a back seat here
Family glosses over flaws
Sometimes our beloved family
Includes feathers, hooves, or paws

The outside world soon will fade
To step indoors, like welcoming shade
A place to soothe the body and soul
I will have some rest and then a stroll

I walk down the peaceful road
I leave behind the world's load
The sun is setting and so am I
My walk is ending with home nearby

Sometimes home is just for you
A heartfelt comfort all your own
God and angels watch over you
To make sure you are not alone

Home sweet home

Summoned to the Hills

The flowers summoned her to appear
They directed her to a certain hill
To help her through a troubling time
Where time seemed to stand still

It was an awkward time in her life
Where time stood still and brought great pain
She longed to get back to the place
Where she could see him again

The flowers told her "Separation brings pain
But it also makes your love grow stronger
We want to reassure you dear
Soon you will be alone no longer
The man you love is doing work
What he feels, he is not handling well
He was not looking for love when he found you
His mind is troubled, he is under your spell
His heart has feelings he cannot hide
He is working to be well inside
He is a strong man; you know that too
He is unfamiliar with love or what to do
He has been his own man for so many years
He is softening, we saw him show a few tears
Now work on yourself while time seems still
Heartache is a bitter pill
Do your nails and fix your hair
Exercise and give your body care

When the time is right and moves for you
You will look your best, you always do
Try to stop living in the pain
It is part of the process
You are sane
A few of us flowers will travel with you
You can write something beautiful
For something to do
By the way
Keep him in your head
One day you will have him in your bed

Heart Strings

Heart strings tear and loose they lay
Ways are parted, she has gone away
He has gone too, it had to be
He has his own life, he is free

A memory comes to her mind
The kind she does not want to find
The thoughts of him make her heart ache
Heart strings tear when there is a break
Her eyes will well and there is a gaze
To nothingness on certain days
She will sit sometimes for hours
While wind chimes sound, she stares at flowers

Melancholy and loneliness
She looks lovely in her dress
Her thoughts of looking into his eyes
What she felt, it slowly dies

A sad and lonely end it brings
A broken heart and torn heart strings
There is a secret she does not know
He did not want to let her go
He misses her even more
Soon he will be at her door
They both have heart strings to mend
They have a love that cannot end

Fig Tree Generation

It is time to separate the figs
Good fig, bad fig, good fig, bad
There are too many bad figs now
Too many bad figs, Lord, it is sad

The good figs though few are exceptionally good
The bad are so bad they have no use
The bad are still hanging on the tree
It is time to cut the bad figs loose

Bad figs hanging on our tree
Does not help the tree at all
Dear Lord, it is time to cut the bad figs off
Then the bad figs cannot cause good figs to fall

Bad figs Lord, they are bad, bad, bad
Right now, it seems past time to pick
Lord, you better send more help
Before the bad figs get too thick

God's Warrior

The blistering heat does not burn his feet
He stomps the fires as he goes along
The devil's own cannot slow him down
He is fighting evil and everything wrong

His boots are made of fortitude
His gloves are filled with hands of steel
The armor God gives him to wear
Gives Satan's thugs real pain to feel

His big boots are kicking pedophiles asses
His hands of steel are punching child porn glasses
He is killing them, they are not going home
They will stop killing children for adrenochrome

The ruling elite, he is putting to death
He is ripping out tongues with his bare hands
The lies they forced upon the masses
Are going to stop right where he stands

He is exposing the hidden dynasties
The one world system and all the lies
With the hammer of God, he is pounding hard
As they are going down you can hear their cries

He walks through evil like he owns it
He is delivering justice and rightly so
He will not abide any evil

It all needs to go
God gave him more warrants He had sealed
God put him to work when He found him kneeled
He is harvesting evil and what a yield
God needs more like him
Working in His field

Finding Sheep

In that dark and cloudy day
God will search out His own sheep
He knows where they all are
Some are lost, some are asleep
Some are broken, and they rest
Some have been driven away
God will gather them to His good pasture
Where they and their good shepherd will stay
In the pasture of God's own flock
All will know their shepherd's voice
When he has His own together
They will all praise God, they will all rejoice

Chocolates

This is a beautiful box of chocolates
They look so perfect, I love the creams
I find them so tempting and...did I say so tempting
They look better real than in my dreams
Little paper cups they are nestled in
I look them over while wearing a grin
Calories do not count if no one else sees
I will choose every single one as I please
I will just eat them one by one
Eating chocolates is delicious fun
When they are gone...hmm...the box is done
Chocolates or dieting? The chocolates won

Frank and that Smell

An unfortunate accident, she is in assisted living
As soon as she is well, she is going to escape
She hears Lynyrd Skynyrd's song "That smell" say you fool you
The hell with this place and all the red tape

Now the staff is looking at her sitting in her chair
Shaking her head from side to side as if she is saying no
But it is Lynyrd Skynyrd's song "That smell" that is playing in her head
Some of the greatest lead guitar music she just can't let go

She still remembers Frank the puppy she loved
Everyone loved Frank, he was the greenhouse dog
She smiles when she remembers his bad habit of farting
You could not hear it, but the smell left a fog

"Can't you smell that smell" were the lyrics for Frank
She felt Lynyrd Skynyrd's song "That smell" was his song
She only ever loved a few dogs in her life
Now the staff is staring at her and wondering what is wrong

She is smiling as a few tears fall from her eyes
Frank was not her dog, but she loved him for real
She did not have many people in her life
Frank made her laugh, he had a special feel

"Can't you smell that smell" were the lyrics
Oh sure, the center here has smells too
But these smells here don't make her laugh
Like Frank's when the girls all squealed PU

Her favorite song and favorite dog Frank
She remembers the treats he liked to be fed
And as far as the staff just staring at her
It is her little secret what is inside her head

Drunkenness

Mushy gushy words
Can spill out when you are drunk
The next day you hope the other party
Was also drunk as a skunk
Hopefully, they do not remember
The mushy words you said
It is possible if they remember
You may experience dread
Wine is a bibbler
It bibbles and blabs
Over exaggerated feelings
Your drunken mouth gabs
Beer is a brawler
Watch what you say
Your mouth may help put you
In a bad, bad way
Bibbles and blabs
And brawlers and jabs
Too much wine or beer
Too much to drink
Mind what you think
Do not let your mouth be your rear

Autumn Love

When I am in mid-autumn trees
Little can compare to these
In their season of colorful glory
Now bits of glory
Falling to the ground
Glory falling all around

If love could replace these leaves
And fall so beautifully then
Lord please
Let love share this autumn story
Let love have the same or more glory
As the leaves

Autumn is the season to fall in love
When two can be warmed with love's embrace
When the chilly air puts color in your face
When the trees become bare
And love encourages kissing
And the two begin missing
Each other's touch
So many leaves, Lord the glory of such
Change some leaves to love
Let them fall and touch
Me

He is in Love

He is in love, he wants her
He wants her to be his wife
Maybe not really his wife
He knows he wants her
In his life
He wants her to be his own
He wants her to share his throne
His house, his life, his thoughts, his bed
He cannot seem to get her out of his head
He is in love
That love is real
That is how true love does feel

Eternal Love

When the silver cord doth part
Alas, no mortal broken heart shall plague
The pained tormented mind
God's all-encompassing love will find
My sanity once more
As mortal hearts love fades away
The most glorious love
Will heal and stay
Lord, you made the mortal heart
Though sometimes it can break apart
At times, the love it gives, rejected
Vulnerable and not protected
Love can be forever lost
It comes with a painful cost
Then
When not looking, it will be there
The greatest love that two can share
It will overflow a heart
And when the silver cord doth part
Your love Lord, will heal and stay
For the one who is here
And the one that went away

For Me

Light of Christ shine
    Victory is thine
You paid a painful fine
    You suffered a painful death for me
For me Lord
    For me Lord
No greater love
    No greater love
To lay your life down
    To Lay it down
Now my life is thine
    Your salvation mine
I give my life to thee
    You laid yours down for me
Light of Christ Shine
    Victory is thine
You paid a painful fine
    Now salvation is mine

Hearts Hide Scars

The more the scars, the stronger the heart
That is what sets the warriors apart
Lost love and rejection are now like stars
Some scars were wounds, and some were wars
They seem to show themselves at night
When you are alone, they come to the light
Like stars, those memories are so far away
When God's light shines, they cannot stay
Like a faint memory a scar may remain here
Like stars that see light
With God, scars disappear

Underworld War

We are in a war yet, so few know
Of silenced voices down below
Underworlds not known to man
Try to imagine if you can
Our military is warring deep
Secrets, tunnels tried to keep
Cities dwelling below the earth
We will see to what Satan gave birth
What will the evil secrets reveal
A disgusting pain we all will feel
Some secrets we will have to see
Are going to change both you and me
There are some innocents rescued here
The evil ones killed so we will not fear
Pray to God for understanding
And strength as the underworld is dis-banding
Pray for those who fight this fight
Pray that they come home all right

She's Surfacing

She is surfacing again
Where she has been, others do not know
She submerges, she goes away
She comes back when her mind wants to stay
She journeys to where secret messages are given
She feels compelled and her mind goes where driven
Though wherever she goes, she does not lose sight
Of whom has always been her guiding light
Some believe she is mentally ill
She does not admit it or take a pill
Life is real and she has a way
To make it through another day
Where she goes, she sees faces
Things are happening in unknown places
And when she surfaces and is in the light
Her pen is calling, and she must write
People do not know her and do not understand
God is guiding the pen in her hand

Rabbit Talk

Out in the flowers, in the Queen Anne's lace
A little gray rabbit with an adorable face
She said, "little bunny, what are you doing here?"
The bunny looked up and said "oh my dear
Do you know how much you and I love God?"
She said, "yes, I do," as she gave a soft nod
She said "every day I walk through the flowers
Sometimes, I sing to God for hours
I let God know I am here to serve
I know He gives me more than I deserve"
The bunny said "God hears the songs you sing
Your joyful noise and the talks you bring
The time you give Him everyday
He wants a blessing to come your way
God said thank you for talking to Him
Prayers from others are getting slim
A special message because you care
He said you will hear His message
When you find a gray hare"

Time Travel

I remember the games I played as a child
I remember the old phones that we dialed
I remember the times we ate decent food
A new neighbor called every male, a dude
The streets we walked were ours to walk
When kids got together, we could really talk
We sat in old cars that did not run
We pretended to drive, to us that was fun
We did not know we were poor
Most everything was second hand that we wore
The older we grew, we noticed these things
Being poor and what a drunken dad brings
The shame that falls on a family's name
As we grew older, we felt the shame
Why was his shame ours to bear?
But judgement, like used clothes to wear
We were called a lot of names
We were victims of other peoples' games
The nights turned wild and so did we
We rarely were together as a family
Dudes and chicks were all we knew
We all smoked, we all drank brew
Sad things happened in the neighborhood
I really do not remember anything good
I wish I knew then what I know now
That by chance some way and maybe somehow

I could rise above the family shame
For things I should have had no blame
The shame I felt had caused a loss
But I was on the road to the cross
Every step I stepped upon that road
Led me to the place where Christ's love showed
I will keep the memories when times were kind
And I will leave the bad ones on the road behind

Flower Zone

Flowers, flowers everywhere
Some were here and some were there
Any place where they were not
She would put them in a pot

She was in the flower zone
There are more like her, she is not alone
Oh look! There are more flower shops
You know she had to make more stops

All the little cups of flowers
Turned into big colors of showers
It is an addiction and there is no fix
She had to make another mix

Behold all her beautiful flowers
A labor of love, so many hours
It is in her blood and when she is done
She admires them all, to her that is fun

Long Summer

Summer nears its end
Relief settles in as we send
The long summer on its way
Oh yes, blessed relief
As we welcome Autumns stay
Go away summer, go away
You can be cruel
Like a bully at school
You cannot beat us down
Any more this year
You are on your way out
I will not shed a tear
Go away summer, go away
You were like a guest
Who overstayed their welcome
Go away summer, go away

Locked Up Hearts

Locked up hearts with rusty locks
Inside hearts where no one knocks
Tough exteriors though they are real
There are hearts that want to feel
True love always finds a way
To seep in farther everyday
It melts rust and finds a key
To open hearts that are love free
Dear heart open, now for me
I am love I need to be
I need a heart where I can grow
Hearts are made for love you know
Love is knocking on your heart
Let the lock on your heart part
Your tough exterior can soften now
Love does that to hearts...somehow

No More Politics

It is true, I have given up on politics
Lies abound in the political realm
I will just keep my eyes on God
I follow the power at the helm

Though politicians have a salary
It is not enough; they want yours too
They fill their bank accounts with millions
While your dollar bills remain just few

I am endlessly solicited
For money, they beg "help us now"
I will just buy something for myself
I will not be a political cash cow

Politics is a fake world, it is not real
Do like I did, walk away
Put your faith and trust in God
Try it, life is better that way

Sparkling Snow

Looking out at a winter's night
Seeing the sparkling ice glitter on snow
What a heavenly remarkable sight
Moonlight makes the snow glitter glow
Twinkles and sparkles top the snow
Some places have a whole sheen of shine
It is as if the angels handed it to me
And said it was theirs but now it is mine
I love a beautiful winter scene
If I could paint it, it would keep
This winter night vision of what I see
Will fade with time like a dream in my sleep

She Changed

She saw her reflection
Though she, herself, could not be found
The spirits of fermented liquid
Turned her upside down
And painfully
Regret once again
She had to hide her face
She put the liquid spirits down
No more to see that place
It was self-inflicted
The pain she felt for her own choices
She forsook her rightful place
She answered the wrong voices

What she felt was unexplained
More painful than correction
She knew she disappointed God, to her
She went the wrong direction
Though her infractions were but small
She felt on a large scale
What she did troubled her heart
She did not like to fail
Forgiveness Lord, redeems a mind
It gives relief to a soul
And just between you and me Lord
It is good to be in control

Wild Hearts

I am off to where the wild birds fly
I will live beneath a bigger sky
Near hills that roll, I will take a stroll
And I may find a stream nearby

I will watch the deer that walk and graze
I will look for paths on sunny days
To see life wild, I am beguiled
To live with nature and its ways

I will take time to stop and pray
I will thank God for life, this wild way
Where few feet go, and wild hearts know
They belong and now must stay

Something in my heart stays wild
It has been there since I was a child
A longing to escape to this living
Where what I see, I feel God giving

And when I die, no fancy fare
Where I die, just bury me there
My spirit gone, wild hearts live on
Wild hearts go back to God when gone

Words from Leaves

I walked to the house under the trees
The leaves were rustling, I heard a moment please
I thought I heard words; I thought it absurd
That was when all the sentences were heard

I heard God is not the author of confusion
His anger is growing with the gender delusion
How did the people become so beguiled?
The sex I appointed at conception defiled

Satan is busy with his hellish plan
Man parts, he is a woman, woman parts a man
God did not create any gender confused
Satan is deceiving them, their minds are abused

Now endless genders and God is not amused
Those who support Satan's lies will soon be excused
That is what happens when you leave God's side
Satan sees your thumb out and gives you a ride
But you do not know where it is going or where it will end
Satan's gender agenda, it is to hell my friend

I told the trees you startled me
When you started to speak
The leaves said we will see you
When you mow the lawn again next week

Going Down

A nation spoils, internal rot
God forsaken and now He is not
Gloom and doom, its only reward
Justice will come with God's swift sword
Vengeance is God's to a nation astray
Hatred for Him and you will pay
What's right is wrong, what is wrong is right
Bizarre new teachings spread like blight
A wicked land with wicked ways
There is no good when no one prays
You changed God's laws, you changed His ways
You banned His word
You are out of days
If someone could find a Bible today
And a few people read it and bow to pray
And if a few more seek for God's face you will find
That more will join and leave their ways behind
Then God will hear you and heal your land
It is getting late, do you understand

Falling Rain, Blowing Kisses

It is falling now
The rain
It has been absent
Almost non-existent
A person can forget
What rain is like
The sight of it
The feel of it
The smell of rain falling
Sometimes it smells like the river
Not so fresh
But still fresh
No rain brings a longing inside
A despair
An internal draught
Some people are walking in it
To re-unite with it
Some people blew kisses up
And thanked God
More people should blow kisses up
And thank God
It is falling now
The rain

Freedom Train

I was riding along on the freedom train
I was getting thrown off and I was not home yet
The conductor said "see if you can help these people"
It was something I know I will not forget
He threw me off at the raging river
There was no water but a river of people screaming
I turned around with my fingers in my ears
I turned around again, and oh dear, I was not dreaming
Screaming and yelling and a lot of red faces
Some were proficient putting vulgar words through their paces

All this raging and I was sure I knew the fix
So, I screamed out myself and yelled "Is it politics?"
Wow, it got quiet, and someone yelled your dime
We will see if you can tell the truth, if not you will lose your time
I said I used to feel what you feel, I had mental pain
Politics and politicians nearly drove me insane
Most lie and beg for money, and they do not fix a thing
I let go of politics and the headaches it can bring

Now I ride the freedom train, I do not hear what they say
It does not matter what party they are, they all beg the same way
The best medicine I have for you is my advice and it is free
Stop watching news on mainstream media, your phones, and your TV
The same few people own the media, and they promote fake news
Brainwashing you into what to believe, distortions and their views

A few screamers got worked up and they began to yell
I said wait, and I can tell you how to put them all through hell
No more donations! No money!
Do not give any money at all
They are paid by our tax dollars so let the bad ones fall
They were voted in, and they can be voted out
No more money for politics, that is what I am talking about

Hurry everyone, hear the whistles, see the freedom trains
No politics or politicians, no media for brain washed brains
People looked in awe at one another from the words I had to say
I said freedom trains are free to ride and you can board today
It is true that just hearing the truth can set some people free
The few that did not want to board just stood and stared at me
The raging people now had relief, happily boarding the trains
Those not boarding stood scratching their heads
That held their brain washed brains

Driftwood and Diamonds

He was hardened like a piece of driftwood
Washed up from circumstances
Brined and cured in the waters of life
Fortune never offered him any chances

He has washed up on different shores
Only to be taken back out with the flow
Until she found him and called him a treasure
She found her driftwood when the waters were low

There is a process to create rare driftwood
Some will go out and seek it like gold
He was driftwood and found by a diamond
Value is in the eyes that behold

She could see deeper because she was a diamond
Diamonds begin forming when they are still coal
All the pressures of a bad life refined her
Now driftwood and a diamond share the same soul

Both had been tried and refined by the earth
Driftwood and diamonds can both have great worth
Both had other origins at their core
Now happily ever after, they do not see the before

Race to Win

Life is a foot race, you race to win
There will be obstacles to overcome sin
Hurdles to jump and batons to hand on
You cross the finish line, then you are gone
The crowd is cheering, you won the race
Everyone in heaven now sees your face
The trophy you ran for is given to all
Eternal life from God
When Jesus died for us all
You accepted Jesus when you entered the race
You won eternal life with the help of God's grace

Some Books Do Not Open

Some people have an unknown story
A life of their own they keep inside
Some things need to be protected
And kept from others and they will hide
Some things need to stay in the shadows
Not to share or let others find
You never know who you will meet next
So let your words be kind

The First Earth Age

It was the most beautiful and far away time
All the trees praised God who created them
They were all singing a heavenly chorus
Then one of the trees grew an ungodly stem

The tree's stem protruded, and others took notice
The wicked stemmed tree became quite the hellion
He persuaded a third of the trees to follow
To rise above God and cause a rebellion

God said "who dost thou think thou art wicked tree?"
How dare you try to be greater than me
God's furious anger ignited and spilled
Never! No more would that world age be filled

God removed His children, His trees
He took them out of the first earth age
The beautiful world He created was now gone
Blackness was now that earth's age stage

God destroyed the first earth age
The rebellion caused a furious rage
The firmament destroyed crashed to the ground
Not one single living cell of life to be found

Then the beautiful age was gone
Satan's rising brought a great fall
All those who resisted Satan's rising
Were now God's chosen, He protects them all

It Will

If night falls
    And it will
And if a mating bird calls
    And it does
And if fire burns
    And it will
And if love comes along
    And it might
And if love goes away
    And it could
Then life will go on
    And it will
If you let love live again
    It will
And if it be your will to love
    You will
Then life will go on again
    And it will
You will find it will

Winter Fog

It was dark outside but there was a special beauty
There was fog in the night
The fog stayed throughout most of the day
The day chose not to give light

The fog in the freezing air touched all of nature
It covered all of nature with pure delight
Everything was covered with flocked crystals like a blanket
Everything was dressed in wintery white

Beauty is not always captured with sunshine
Today the day chose to sleep and dream
At times fog and flocked trees perform magic
And they can outshine a sunbeam

Bye-Bye Burger Joint

I am glad I stopped eating there a long time ago
Since we found their burgers contained human meat
At times I felt ill after I ate their food
I hope I never ate human legs or feet
Or ribs, arms, butts, or backs
I went through the drive thru for the brown paper sacks
I wonder how many people were killed
For them to get their meat quotas filled
Inspectors found human meat, with great fears
I hope I never ate human thighs or ears
Or shoulders, ankles, hands, or eyes
I wonder what dreadful things they did to their fries
Worm meat, then horse meat, now human flesh
I will just stay home and make everything fresh

Waterfalls

Waterfalls, where the water falls
From heights above to depths below
Higher to deeper
More powerful when steeper
All of them put on a show
Some are inviting, some can be frightening
Some waterfalls are man made
Some fall to places to splash back on faces
Where those who love waterfalls wade
Watching waterfalls in slow motion
Surely could lull me to sleep
Others so heavenly and so beautiful
They will keep falling, in the memories I keep

Live for Good

Darkness is fading
The night is gone
The morning sun rises
The day is new
Joy cometh in the morning
Another day
To want good
To find good
To live for good
The Lord is good
He is our joy

Their Very First Kiss

A feeling went through her whole body
Everything in her life now felt whole
She knew for certain; he was hers now
His kiss went to her heart and soul
She waited her whole life for this moment
She felt it could happen
But
Could it happen to her?
When twin flame soulmates kiss
For the first time
Would they really be in love?
Yes
They were

Dreaming

The sharks were underneath the ice
The ice was thick, but I felt fear
You see if I fell through the ice
The sharks would gobble me up, oh dear

It was dark and I was on a ship
The waters were raging, and I felt fear
One wrong move and I would fall in
And I knew there must be sharks lurking near

Then a white tiger had my arm in its mouth
It did not bite hard, but it held my arm tight
Suddenly! there were more tigers
But somehow, I got away all right

Last night I pulled out three of my teeth
It did not hurt, but now my teeth had a hole
How in the world can my mind find these dreams?
While I do not seem to have any control

I am tired and I need some sleep
But how can I sleep with scary things
Wild animals and raging deep waters
Concealed messages my hidden mind brings

I would rather dream of love and flowers
Beautiful sights and soft rain showers
Could I not be doing something right
To dream of unsettling things in the night

From now on when I go to bed
I will fill my thoughts with God instead
From now on I will not forget to pray
And the scary things will stay away

Light in the Fog

In the fog I can see my way through
There is a light that my soul can see
And when I focus on that light
That light reaches out to me

With gentle persuasion I follow
The light of Christ surrounds me
It pulls me to the source of his power
Where my heart and soul and eyes can see

No fog or darkness can separate me
Or block my way, there will always be
A light to shine in the fog of the day
With that love light, God guides my way

The light was given for all to see
And I chose to follow the light

The Visit

She went for a visit to those hidden hills
She made a pilgrimage to her hiding place
She had a meaningful conversation
With a wildflower with a beautiful face
She said "I love him, though he does not know
I try hard not to let my feelings show
It is getting harder every day
I love him in an overwhelming way"

The flower said "your love is deep
The greatest love that is meant to keep
Practice patience and stay by his side
His love he will give and with you abide
You only know one side of the story
You see dear, you are missing some pages
His love is growing, and he wants you also
Believe me, I know all the stages"

The flower said "your chosen birds
The ones that you turn into words
Keep them in your hand for now
Soon you will hear him make a vow
Then release a few of those birds
Give them to him in heartfelt words
This love, like flowers will bloom that day
You will find true love is here to stay"

The flower said "you just be you
A plan is unfolding, it is nearly through
He loves you now
He always will
Now you go write
Climb another hill

Digital Warriors

There were those who thought she was weird
She tells them things they have never heard
She is grateful for the digital warriors
Who investigate the evil and absurd

They are talented dark web warriors
They go where others do not go
They fight to get out truthful information
They feel good people need to know

They fight with digits and war with codes
They expose evil and all it abodes
In war rooms or at night with kids in their beds
They see things they do not want in their heads

She tries to get the information out
People do not understand what she is talking about
Conversations are brief and she gets cut off
They shake their heads and of course they scoff

She snickers seeing them stuck in their ruts
Watching fake news with their heads in their butts
The fake news keeps people busy with lies
She is watching them watch their own demise

Digital warriors she is on your side
Learning the truth has been a great ride
It is a war your minds and fingers can bring
With a keyboard you expose every evil thing

In the darkness or in the light of day
This weird lady will watch and pray
She is waiting for all the truth to come out
Then others will know what she was talking about

They do not know what is going on
Her friends tell her what is on the fake news
She does not know what they are talking about
When they repeat the fake news and its deceitful views
Hmm.... just wondering who is crazy

Flying High

I can fly like an eagle today
I belong to God and when I pray
He hears my words
He knows every thought
He feels my love
And me, He sought
And found
I will bless God with all I own
With my own words
With the seeds I have sown
And when I am done praying
God will show me a way
Where I can fly as high
As an eagle today

I Am Who I Am

I cannot be what you want, dear friend
If I changed for you
It would be my end
The me I know would go away
Sadly, sadly
Friends are few
I am who I am
And that is my view

You should overlook my flaws, dear friend
You cannot change my will
Though yours could bend
If I change my will for you to okay
Surely my spirit will break that day
Sadly, sadly
Friends are few
I am who I am
And that is my view

I have a friend who stays by my side
I do not have to change
Or my feelings hide
Unconditional love he gives to me
Forgiveness and grace, these gifts are free
Gladly, gladly he is mine
I am who I am
And he thinks I am fine

Hall of Same

Everything was the same in the hall of same
Same seconds, same minutes, same hours, same days
Everything the same in all the same ways
Where are the windows or doors to get out
What was the "hall of same" all about?

Finally, a change in the hall of same
I could not take it anymore
And I said my name
I said it over and over and I said God's name too
I said Lord I need something new to do
A thought was thought
And I began to pray
It was time to see the same old thing go away
Out with the same and in with the new
A new door opened; it was time to go through
Places to go and people to see
No more would the same old thing be for me

Though one thing for me will always be the same
My love for God and the power of his name
He was making a way to set me free
All the while I was working on me

Seasons Change

Seasons change
As do I
My wings unfolding
I must fly to higher heights
Above the lows
Where I go the Lord God knows
His seasons change
With gentle calling
Wings of faith keep me from falling
Through all God's seasons
He was with me
Passing through seasons
To find one for me

Bad Job Work Week

Death's door
It is only Tuesday
Usually, you visit on Thursday
Sometimes Friday, mid-day
I live again on Saturday
Starting Friday night
Tuesdays are for misery
Do not force Tuesday
To handle deaths door

Truth, Light, Love

When you bring truth to light
A new light shines
And with love it grows

When you bring love to light
It attaches and it shines and grows
It heals and spreads and makes a way
For darkness not to touch the day

Love is a gift and a light to shine
Truth to light
God's love is mine

Love Words

Gilded words of love
Spoken from the heart
Those words cherished
Like a finely wrapped gift
A keepsake for the soul
Held close will not part

Thinking Process

I had thoughts
And after thoughts
Thoughts, thoughts, thoughts
And too much thinking, and over thinking
Thinking thoughts to have a drink
Then I thought I did too much drinking
I think when drinking, thoughts are few
Thinking thoughts that are askew
You fail to think before you speak
Tomorrow comes and my thoughts and I
Seek to hide
I am better off
Thinking thoughts and after thoughts
And over thinking
Over thinking is far less painful
Yes, less painful than over drinking

Somewhere

Somewhere there is a place
Where I would like to go
I do not know where it is
Though, it is there I know
Hidden for right now
I see it through a haze
I cannot quite make it out
I see glimpses on some days
I know it is a wonderful place
I know I will love it there
I just know I must find it
I know it is there somewhere

The Right Road

Lord,
Help me stay on the straight road
A winding road causes weariness
The wide road is busy and leads to destruction
A forked road can put you on the wrong path
Help me stay on the straight and narrow road
The road where few go but the reward is great
At times it is a lonely and tedious road
But it will take me to heaven's gate

We are Only Human

God said be holy for He is holy
Though you do not have to be a holier than thou
People self- righteous and self- appointed judges
Can get on God's nerves somehow
We all have sinned and fallen short of God's glory
Some have slipped and gone astray
Some have lost their grip on God's guiding rod
But they will come back when they find their way
God said ask and He will forgive your sins
Christ paid the price with His life on the cross
Do not self-appoint yourself judge and jury
Or you will be judged yourself and may suffer loss
Do not walk around with your nose in the air
Like everyone else, you also sin
Jesus went into the publicans and sinners
And He was welcomed in
You see, we are all only human
Do not act like you are the same as God
You may wear His patience thin
And he might bop you with His guiding rod

Poor Harvest

The sky was growing dark
There was a harvest to be had
Not for crops but for souls
Oh my, the crop was bad
There was a harvest, what a mess
It was full of chaff
It was taken to God's thresher
To be beaten with his staff

The crop that made it was healthy and strong
But the chaff only lived for themselves
That was wrong

Every evil dis-order was theirs
No room for God, his love, or his cares
Never a prayer or thought for their maker
There were no givers, everyone a taker
Selfish and self-centered, greedy and liars
The threshers were beating and removing the briars
Killing babies in the womb
Child raping
Sexual deviants would not be escaping

The lies, oh the lies that were forced on humankind
There would be no lenience they would find

God gave his son Jesus who paid the price
He offered forgiveness
But they never thought twice
To accept the gift God gave and it was free
Off to the threshing floor
Your deeds
The threshers will see

Wrong Love

She was putting her lower self on
She would be wearing that version till dawn
Looking for love where it did not exist
Looking for feelings she could not resist
Giving her true self away for love
Giving her true self away
She did not have someone to love
She tried to find it the wrong way

Whatever it takes
Those were mistakes
Whatever it takes to feel
Love that is not truly real

Love is not found in sex for the night
Giving yourself away is not right
You lose your true self and hide your light
When your lower self and your higher self fight

Now put that lower self away
Look to God and humbly pray
You can pray and if you believe
He answers prayers, then you can receive
True love
You will receive true love

Watching Him

I was looking at him
He usually did not have a care in the world
Now, he was complaining
Trying to get help over the phone
You could tell by the conversation
He was not getting helped
He wanted answers
I saw glimpses of him in his younger years
I saw his younger self manifest
He was giving someone hell
Rightfully so
I was amazed at his morphing
I did not know him when he was that age
Now I saw the whole man
The young man and the silver
He was not old
He had been tried
And he was pure silver

Let God Move

Resist the temptation to move yourself
A greater power will move for you
Others do not have to understand
When you do things the way you do

The hearts wisdom is doing something
The mind cannot understand
The mind and the heart will war with each other
But the heart has the upper hand

The upper hand that comes from God
He moves in ways we do not know
He moves obstacles and creates new paths
He will make a better way to go

When time creates a void in your life
Let God work, stay who you are
Life moves fast and slow at the same time
It moves like fluid, water, or tar

Time brings patience and you can pray
Align yourself with God every day
Let your hearts intuition guide your way
Listen to God, not what others have to say

Caution: Foxes

The foxes trotted away from the vines
They frolicked in the grapes tended for wines
Their careless play caused good fruit to fall
They also broke vines and that is not all
They were tricky
They pretended to be friends
They take you down sneakily
Then do not make amends
They like spreading rumors and
Betraying "said" friends
One tells lies while the other tends the spreading
Dirty little foxes, laying in their dirty bedding
Foxes are self-centered
They are very tricky
They like to make messes that tend to be sticky
You cannot trust a fox to be your friend
They will trample the grapes that you live for and tend
Be wiser than a fox when someone new
Seems desperate to be friends with you

The Light

Above the clouds in the sky at night
Cloud edges glow with a radiant light
All around me as I fly
Stars glisten gracefully
As I pass by
Where am I going tonight?
To the light that beckons me to come?
To the light that calls the chosen some?
It was so beautiful, God's own show
The light is calling, I must go
I fly to the light that knows my name
It knows me, I came from the same
I was traveling to the glorious light
On such a blissfully beautiful night
So heavenly I felt I must be dying
Then a voice of love said "you are dreaming"
So, I kept flying
To the light

Blackbird Good-byes

I felt a few tears in my eyes
As I heard the blackbirds sing their good-byes
Fall was in session, the air was cold
God was gathering them to leave
They were told
Hearing the thousands of blackbirds' cry
We are leaving soon, good-bye, good-bye
Sadness was setting in my heart
As I watched the blackbirds gather to part
They gather by the thousands
Before they fly
Thank you, dear blackbirds
For saying good-bye
In their calling I heard sadness
And excitement as well
I wished it were me leaving
And saying farewell
Being excited for a new life
And something new to try
I will see you again, blackbirds
When I see the spring sky

P's and Q's

We were told to mind our P's and Q's
You can mind the P's, I will take the Q's
You put a U behind the P
You get PU I will take the Q
I like the Q's because they need U's
And we know Q's and they need us
I am on the Q and us bus
You cannot have quantum without the q
You cannot have quantum without the u
The Q's have quadrants
And quandaries to quicken
And queries and quests
Now the plot thickens
They have quagmires to quash
They have qualms to quell
They have quality quakes
Sending evil ones to hell
Q's have quadrillions
And that is a lot
Do I want a P?
They have their place
And a use but
No, I think not

Baggy Bottoms

What is wrong with you, pull up your pants
Did they just slide below your underwear by chance?

Do you know how to use a tape measure?
Is underwear showing on your butt a pleasure

What is going on, are you a slob
You could not wear those pants to a decent job
Get yourself a job and make some good money
Looking at underwear butts is not funny

Measure your waist and buy the right size
Give some relief to other peoples' eyes

Wear the right size pants, it will help you look smart
You will also have another layer of protection
When you fart

Self-Centered

Yes, I read the article
It was in the newspaper today
It said the world revolved around you
We must all make your day
It said you were the most important
We need to respect your feelings
We need to watch our words with care
In all your daily dealings
We need to mind the looks on our faces
We need to hang on to your every word
We need to make you the center of attention
We need to know everything you heard
Your parents should be charged with a crime
For raising you that way
Self-centered and the world revolves around you
Am I revolving around you?
No way
Open your eyes, be mindful of others
We are all the same in this human race
Try looking at others for a change
You will find yourself in a better place

Swallow Stream

She was crossing Swallow Stream
All you could see was a hand holding a book
She was traveling to the hidden hills
To show the flowers and let them look
Swallow Stream had the appearance of being shallow
Though instantly water was over her head
She was persistant, she was going to make it
Under water she heard the words the stream said
Swallow Stream said I hate to babble like a brook
I just thought you might like a few words for your book
It spoke
At times you felt like you were drowning
So many times, life's waters were deep
Often troubles overwhelmed you
Just to encounter hills too steep
But dear, you are an overcomer
Circumstances never keep you down
Like your book in your hand, God protected you
You always surface with no tarnish on your crown
She said thank you Swallow Stream
For your heartfelt words
Though I like to eat fish
I prefer to catch birds

Scandalous Rumors

It was scandalous, a price will be paid
For the lies that were told, for the rumors that were made
Gossip put on its shoes and ran to the track
Ran around all the way till the rumor got back
It had some words it just had to spill
To see it in other eyes brought a great thrill
Facts were in the back seat, they were not known
There were too many dogs carrying a bad bone
A life can be ruined, a job can be lost
When someone spreads rumors, there is a cost
A true love can end forever and all time
When rumors are spread on gossips dime
Words were not repeated in the manner that they should
The rumor gets bigger, exaggeration is not good
Eyes are looking around to see the rumor through
Beware my friend, the eyes may be on you

Law of Attraction

Exchanging the pleasantries of the day
He certainly had a unique way
Of looking at her
She took notice and felt a stir

She blushed
When the blood rushed
To more than just her face

"What are you doing to me?"
She mis-spoke
Though she clarified with
"I meant, what are you doing?"
She had a slight choke

He replied "I was just looking at you"
He blushed too, he did
He meant to say "I was just looking for something"
His true feelings he hid

Hmm, they were following the law
The law of attraction

Gifts to Workers

Perfect peace, it is a gift
God will give it when it is due
You can feel it, and know it is His
You have done your work; you have done His too

Another gift is God's sweet rest
He gives it when you have done your best
God loves workers and I find it true
If you are lazy, there is nothing for you

After the Rain

After the rain
Some clouds remain
Birds fly about
Looking for food

I feel God's presence
Rain is a blessing
He causes it to fall
On the bad and the good

God gives rain
It nourishes life
Like food for the soul
Everything grows

The rain falls on all
Though I pray for more
For me and my friends
And less for my foes

Patriots vs Traitors

Patriotic love for America is deep and real
Patriot hearts bleed loyalty, that is what we feel
Our flag we honor and with respect we stand
For our families who serve to protect our land
The greatest country in the world
Here all races are free
While patriots stand
The traitors take a knee
Freedom rings, under God we are free
A curse to the traitors who take a knee
A curse and damnation
For your fabricated lies
Your racism and socialism
In a sordid disguise
You are hiding evil in a sport uniform
You brought the fight, here comes the storm
There is no place in America for traitors
When you take a knee, you are America haters
You deserve no respect
And we have none for you
Your fan base has dwindled
When you kneel, we will boo
Kneeling traitors wear dishonor and disgrace
It nauseates us to see your face
Traitors are not team players when they make our country worse
You are trading your glory days for a lifetime curse

I would not give sports the time of day
It would not bother me if sports went away
Sport players are overpaid to play with balls
While our real heroes defend you when they receive calls
Sadly, some die earning a military wage
While you rake in money feigning racial outrage
All we have for kneeling traitors is shame
The patriots will win big, traitors will lose the game

Do not Be a Rug

It is OK to fight what is wrong
When Jesus confronted the money changers
He did not sing them a song

He did not softly say "I do not like you doing that"
He threw over the tables
Where the money changers sat

Jesus grabbed a whip, to whip and chase them out
He took care of business
The right way no doubt

They were selling mite infested doves in His Father's house
Jesus put on His kicking boots
He did not act like a mouse

That is a real problem with some followers today
They close their eyes to trouble
And very few pray

They act like little rugs, for crooks to wipe their feet
When they have the power within them
They would rather take a seat

They are so full of fear, they will not stand up to fight
They do not want to speak out
They do not stand for what is right

I belong to God and do everything I can
Where the Lord starts a fire
I will be His fan

I will fan the flames to make evil run
I will help God's fire burn it
You are missing the fun
God is a consuming fire; He has evil to burn
We are God's army
We all take our turn

For some, you are better off just being a little rug
When enemies attack you
You can just give them a hug

What was That?

For a moment, I felt two hearts beating
One was mine, I was alone
I thought I felt a hand touch me
Yet no hand was shown
I thought I heard my name spoken
I heard a knock, and I was woken
From a side view I thought someone was there
I was startled and looked
It was only air
For a moment in time, I saw someone
Maybe our angels are having fun
God's angels are watching over us
They probably shake their heads when we cuss
Maybe they like to mess with our minds
Maybe they would like to kick our behinds
For getting on their nerves and misbehaving
Information they are always saving
For God

I Need a Scarecrow

The first day of Autumn is a few weeks away
Outside, I can feel it in the air today
My heart relieved, leaps for joy for Fall
It is my all-time favorite season of all
Summer's grueling heat has done me in
I am excited and cannot wait for Fall to begin
The special colors, the air, the sights
Windows cracked open to feel the cool nights
I will put out a scarecrow to make summer go away
Yes, I have had enough summer, I do not want it to stay
Long sleeves and sweatshirts are better for me
With leaves changing colors and pumpkins to see
I better get busy; I have work to do
I must make a scary scarecrow
He will be mean too
So mean and scary, it will chase summer away
And make more days for Autumn to stay

Outside Aging

The older I get
The younger I feel inside
Though I feel younger
My wrinkles I cannot hide
Lotions and creams
Facial toners and care
Though I am devout
My wrinkles are still there

I would like to run
But can barely walk- up stairs
I still feel young
While finding lots of gray hairs
My mind is sharper
There is no dementia here
I feel like I am young
But my reflection brings fear

The older I get
And all my outside ages
I still feel young
But cannot read the words on pages
My knees and joints ache
I am getting old, for heaven's sake
And
There is no sorrow
I am God's today and tomorrow
And some tomorrow, God will make me young again

Sparrows

As I look out into the tree
I see movement, it is not the leaves
There are sparrows scattered about
Preening their feathers inside and out

They flit and flutter tails and wings
And to a bird feeder a little one clings
Some hate sparrows at their feeders
I feed the sparrows with all the tweeters

Lord, your eye is on the sparrow
My eyes are on your sparrows too
I love feeding our little birds
Though you feed them, I like to help you

Our hungry birds know where to eat
All the Lord's birds are welcome here
Bird food, shade, and branches to rest
Lord, I find our little sparrows dear

Gift to One Hidden

Twas God's good gift, a pen in my hand
My prayers filled a glass like sand
Among the crowds I felt concealed
Then God sought me
My mind He sealed
I had some thoughts that I revealed
Long ago feelings, now are healed
Oft my pen blazed lightning strikes
I felt God's likes and His dislikes
If not from God words could not be
And when from God the words penned free
I gave my life to God on the throne
God gave me words
Mine and his own

Do not Turn Around

The footprints that I leave behind
They are messy as I turn to see
I thought that I should clean them up
Though I will let them be
The steps behind were toilsome
Burdensome, though I keep going
There is no time to clean past steps
For God's calling, there is no slowing
What I have done and where I have been
Have been hard steps since way back when
Do not point out what I left behind
Most of those steps were not kind
Family, false friends and jobs were trying
Footprints behind can lay there dying
I am on the path: I hear God calling
You will see my footprints, not me falling

Good-bye Hidden Hills

She made one more trip to the hidden hills
To visit the wildflowers and daffodils
She wanted to tell them for heaven's sake
How did she ever let her heart break?

She told them she was so strong inside
She fell and went on a downhill slide
She was not looking but love came her way
It was not expected but it would stay
And not knowing how to grasp these feelings
Caused her heartache and new love dealings
Love found her but she had to wait
Till God prepared a starting date
It was waiting that brought her so much pain
But it also brought tremendous gain

He also knew the flowers well
At times he tried to give them hell
But they would put him in his place
When all the flowers had her face
Those sneaky flowers had a plan
They helped God join this woman and man
She would love him forever more
And he loved her to her very core

Daydreaming took her on a bad trip
It caused her feelings to slide and slip
But reason wakes and takes control
When God corrects a heart and soul
When God brings true love for you to keep
He wakes you out of your unloved sleep
Love that you were not looking for
Can just show up and it wants more

The flowers were so happy to see her face
One said, sometimes God puts us in our place
His love corrects and makes things right
God brought you a man to share your light

Your journey took you all the way
To the place where you are stronger today
Hearts, thoughts, love, and words
We think you caught some beautiful birds
And for visiting us and the flowers you chose
We will always remember you as one of those
Good-bye flowers; thanks for helping me
You were the most beautiful flowers I ever did see
She blew a kiss to the flowers when she said good-bye
Then set her birds free
Forever more to fly

www.ingramcontent.com/pod-product-compliance
Lightning Source LLC
Chambersburg PA
CBHW020309010526
44107CB00001B/45